POEMS AND EXPLANATIONS

Cheeky Monkey HD.com

ISBN: 9798877503878
Imprint: CMHD Publishing

Cover design by: Cheeky Monkey HD.com

INTRODUCTION

(THIS BIT IS NOT A POEM)

Hi Guys, it's me, Cheeky Monkey HD.com, here.
It is a well known fact that poetry is the cleverest, fanciest and hardest of all the art forms known to man. As such, its inherent complexity means that the very notion of poetry is held out far beyond the reach of the normal, everyday guy, such as yourself. That seems something of a shame.

Luckily, unlike you, I, Cheeky Monkey HD.com, am excellent at poetry. I don't say this to brag, show off, nor impress. It's quite simply a bonafide fact. I was born with an incredible, innate talent for the construction of rhymetangles. A built-in penchant to verify verse. A simple, natural tendency to use words good.

Given the enormous heap of luck that has been plonked upon my head - vis a vis poetry - I feel that it is my duty to, not only to share some of my epic verses, but also to explain them in a way that even you will understand. Only then will my parlour feel truly welcoming.

Sit down, take off your shoes and relax:

I. Got. This.

MY PIE

You've eaten my pie
Without my say so
The taste so delicious
Meat and potato
Open your mouth
Teeth in my crust
It all starts to crumble
Just like my trust
The truth is apparent
To share, I was willing
But your selfish approach
Has devoured my filling

Guys, this poem isn't *just* about pies. Sure, there was an occasion when we were having Pie Friday in the office and somebody took the meat & potato that I had *definitely* ordered and I was left with a **pointless** chicken and mushroom pasty (not ***even*** a pie!!). Despite holding a week-long inquest into the matter - in which I offered full immunity from disciplinary action for anyone involved - nobody had the guts to step forward. Pathetic.

But the poem is also about falling in love with someone who doesn't love you back or something equally deep and meaningful. And it's also definitely about the time when you *really* wanted that meat and potato pie.

INAPPROPRIATE KEY

I pull my crayon
Out from the box
I draw a key
To open your locks
It doesn't work
I need an axe
To open your clasps
I need more than wax

This is pretty clever stuff, if I do say so myself. Let's run through some of the key points:
Who uses crayons? Little kids. Who uses axes? Big tough guys with beards. Who has a lock? Anyone who has some valuables to protect. Who says 'clasps'? Probably some mediaeval monk.
Are you with me yet, or do I have to spell it out a bit more?
I do?
OK then:

ITISABOUTBEINGSADINSIDE

CRISPS

You took my potatoes
And stripped off their skin
Finely cut slices
Reveal the crisp 'tis within

Now into the fryer
Smothered in fat
I'm turning golden
What do you think about that?

Out of the oil
In a little wire basket
Give me a shake
I'm yours, if you ask it

Cover me in salt
Cover me in vinegar
Hang on a minute…
It's you, Gary Lineker

It's not Gary Lineker. He's just a metaphor. And he likes crisps.

Garry 'Gazza' Lineker is a renowned good egg, and regularly sticks his head on the line to make uncontroversial comments like: "Being bad to people is bad." Unfortunately, the world is full of silly people who hear what he says and inexplicably reply with something like: "Shut up, Gary Lineker. Just because you never received a yellow card in your whole footballing career doesn't give you the right to wade in on highly contentious political issues like the one in which you insist being bad to people is bad. I'm going to tell Mr Beebee-Sea about you."

I sit on the sidelines and smile sensually to myself, recumbent on my luxury sunlounger, sipping on a non-alcoholic cocktail through a bendy straw. I don't say anything, I don't have to. I simply throw paper planes at the stupid ones (i.e. not Gazza), and when they stop to pick up one of the paper planes that has hit them, they notice that there are some words on it that they can't read because it's all folded up, so they unfold it and discover this poem printed onto its flank. Then they read the poem. Then they grow up.

Marvin Gaye
May
But when put on the spot
He may not

Let's Get it On singer, Marvin Gaye, was found to have 'heard it on the grapevine'. When asked 'what's going on?', he was heard to retort: "Don't worry, I'm 'reet petite'." In this sense, Gaye is being used as a vehicle for ideas. Very much a 'concept car', if you will. By driving Gaye down the boulevard of possibilities, we reveal a hesitance to commit. Should he turn left or right at the traffic light(s) of *your* dreams? Should he go straight ahead towards the car park of tomorrow? Should he stick it in reverse and pray that the traffic officer of yesterday isn't watching? Come on, Marvin. Why aren't you moving, Marvin, it's been on green for ages.

Stop rushing him, will you? He's going to end up driving into the back of that Nissan Micra. Which is also a metaphor.

Incidentally, this is the first poem within the book that hasn't got a title. I'm a little bit crazy, aren't I?

GLORIOUS

One, two, three, four
Come on, baby, say you love me
Five, six, seven times
If you say you love me for an eighth time
I will unleash the full force
Of my Miami Sound Machine
And bring furious vengeance
Against you and your people
For I am Empress Gloria Estefan
Of the Grand Galactic Empire
And I will not be disobeyed

Is Gloria Estefan the commander of a space-faring armada, hell bent on conquering the known universe?

I can't say for sure that she isn't, but I'm going to say no, she probably isn't.

(I'm happy to be proven otherwise. This isn't a hill I'm prepared to die on.)

In this context, the juxtaposition of Miss Estefan and the depiction of her as the malevolent ruler of a power-hungry race of aliens is purely *a bit of fun* and really should be treated as such.

BLACK EYED WE

will.i.am
Not amused
Said Queen Victoria
To the Black-Eyed Pea of a rap guy
But yo majesty
Said the unlikely coach, off of The Voice (UK)
To the miserable monarch
Isn't the quote:
"We are not amused"
What you once said?
Yes
Replied the squat Albert botherer
To the bespectacled hat wearer
But "will.we.are"
Isn't your flipping name.

Given the years in which they both lived - Queen Victoria (1819 - 1901), will.i.am (1975 to present) - it seems unlikely that they met at all, let alone had the conversation above. To you, the lay person, this might seem a bit silly. But wait:

As a highly accomplished poet, I have passed all relevant exams and have in my possession a legally-binding Artistic Licence. This credit-card sized, proof-of-address has been used in this instance to imagine a scenario in which two of my favourite fictional characters could actually, and did actually, meet. You see, it's only by conducting these so-called 'thought experiments' that we are able to titrate a pipette's worth of truth from the Bunsen burner of tomorrow.

THE BEST

"You're simply the best,"
Sang Tina Turner.
"Better than all the rest."

"All the rest of what?"
I replied.
"You're not being very specific."

"Better than anyone,"
She countered.
"Anyone I've ever met."

"If anything, that just raises more questions than answers,"
I sighed.
"But thanks, anyway."

This is no more and no less a tribute to the queen of rock n' soul who we sadly lost (i.e. died) in 2023. I had considered writing a poem called Tuna Tirner, as I thought that it might be a clever way of extracting some *truth*, but while 'tuna' is certainly a word (and a fish), 'tirner' is not.

DIAMONDS

Like a diamond
You shine
You're hard
You're precious

Like Anne Diamond
You presented TV-AM
You presented Good Morning with Anne and Nick
You sometimes appear on The Wright Stuff on Channel 5

It is for these reasons
That I love you:
My diamond

Also
I could sell you for loads of money

Or
You could give evidence in the Leveson Inquiry

The origins and meaning behind this 'lost classic' are somewhat shrouded in mystery, a bit like when the top of Mt. Fuji isn't visible and you go home from your coach trip feeling disappointed. I have absolutely no memory of composing this verse, yet its sheer *poetry* is so profound that it must be one of mine. And it was written in the back of a Panini sticker album in my handwriting, stuck at the bottom of my wardrobe, so it is *deffo* one of mine. I know it must seem crazy to you that someone could write something so amazing and then forget it, but such is the sheer deluge of art that springs forth from my frothy gut.

Anyway, it seemed a shame not to stick it in this book, just to pad it out a bit, if nothing else. Sadly, my complete lack of recollection as to writing it, let alone my motivations for doing so, makes it hard to analyse. What even is this 'Leveson Enquiry' that I mention? It sounds important and it might be relevant to the overall *gist* of the poem, but I've no idea, and I can't be bothered to Google what it was, or why Anne Diamond gave evidence in it.

And it's not even called The Wright Stuff any more, is it? It's called Jeremy Vine, which, if you ask me, just feels lazy. They could have at least called it 'The Vine Stuff'.

Wake up, Channel 5.

SO COOL, SO TIRED

Let's keep a secret, yeah?
Just you and me
Baby, let's go home
And have a cup of tea
When we're together
We're looking so cool, yo
But, girl, we shoulda been home
An hour ago
You're rocking that dress
You're quite the sight
But it's getting kind of late, yeah?
It is a work night
Cos baby, when we're together
Nothing can harm us
So let's get home
And put on pyjamas
When we're together
We're looking so cool, yo
But, girl, we shoulda been home
An hour ago

I'll be honest, this isn't so much a poem as it is lyrics to a song. A few years ago, I was trying to invent a new genre of music called "funkytiredcore" aimed at the underserved 40plus R'n'B fan who can't be bothered going to clubs anymore. Alas, despite having a clear gift for song writing, and, actually, a pretty fantastic singing voice, I have absolutely no capacity for making music, so I got bored and just left it.

The poem appears in this collection as a tribute to my untapped talent. I'm open to someone setting these lyrics to music, but I must insist that in order to do so you've won at least 2 Grammys.

THIS POEM IS BROUGHT TO YOU BY THE LETTER S

Stanley's spaniel, Sally
Sat serenely

Stanley suspected Sally
Sought sausages:
Surreptitiously seeking
Special Sustenance

Sally sighed
She shook skull
Sidey sidey

Silly Stanley
Silly suspicious Stanley
So sad

Sometimes a poet just really needs to show off and prove their poetical might via a highly technical, complex piece of writing. In this case the challenge was: 'start every word in the poem with S'. It's harder than it sounds and it already sounds really hard. It proved a challenge, even for me. I mean, 'sidey sidey' isn't really a thing is it?

And, frankly, a dog is *clearly* always thinking about sausages, so I don't know why I allowed Sally to get up upon her metaphorical high horse about Stanley thinking that she wanted some. Sounds like she's got a bit of an attitude.

That said, why was Stanley so bothered that a dog wanted a sausage? As a dog owner, surely he knows that's par for the course? Dogs are, quite literally, sausage munching machines.

All in all, they sound like a right pair of weirdos. I'm happy to go on record and say that I'll never write another poem about them. I'd just rather not.

THE HELLAVATOR

I'm trapped in a lift
I've tried ringing the bell
This metallic coffin
Will it take me to hell?
When the doors open
Where will I be?
In another dimension
Where my soul can roam free

OH GROW UP.
I've been in a lift loads of times and the most exciting thing that's
ever happened to me is to arrive on another floor.
Just wait for maintenance.
END OF POEM.

Wow, guys... talk about disrupting the form or what? I imagine you're feeling a little overwhelmed by art at this moment in time, so please don't feel embarrassed about putting the book down, making a cup of tea, sitting back in your 'lazy chair' and just BREATHE. I'll still be here when you're feeling better.

Welcome back.

I started with the title "Hellavator" because it seemed like there would be a lot of poetical mileage in the concept of a lift that descended into hell. But when I started writing it, I remembered that we call them 'lifts' not 'elevators' and that started to really annoy me. By the time I got to mentioning 'another dimension', I felt like this person in the lift was pathetic and I wanted to bail on the poem completely, just out of sheer and utter contempt for the protagonist.

I couldn't do that, though, as I have a clear policy of a) completing every poem I start, and b) publishing every poem that I complete. What could I do?

Well, I pulled on my salopettes, pulled down my goggles, and slapped some of that white stuff, that stuff idiot cricketers use, on my nose; that's right, I went off-piste. After that, I simply smashed convention into next week.

CYCLISTS

I've got special equipment
I'm a road user too
Give me my right of way
Give me MY space

I've got special equipment
I'm going to slow you down
But it is my RIGHT of way
You have to give me my SPACE

I've got special equipment
I'm wearing a colourful top
We're riding two abreast now
You have to give me respect

I've got special equipment
WATCH WHERE YOU'RE GOING
The tightness of my shorts
Has cut off circulation to my brain

If this poem appears to be a thinly veiled attack on cyclists, cyclists' ways and cyclists' opinions then you'd be correct. Poetry is not above having petty digs at things that, quite rightly, annoy you.

90'S DANCE DILEMMA

What is Love?
Asked Dr Alban

What is Dr Alban?
Asked Love

Wikipedia intervened:
Encompassing a range of strong and positive emotional and mental states
A Swedish musician and producer with his own record label

Both parties went home happy

There's, *like*, two sides to every coin, isn't there? One side of the coin (the head) is saying "yeah, but what's the tails doing?", whilst the other side of the coin (the tails) is saying "I'm absolutely *sick* of that head, showing off all the time, just because it has facial features".

Guys, if you could just stop for a second, pop out of your side of the coin, walk around the edge and then look at the other side of the coin to the one that you are, then you'd know that they're the same as you.

Except different, obviously.

SISTERS

A grown woman

Allegedly

Acts like a baby

A little baby

Technically the boss

Always right

Has to be her way

When will she learn?

Guys…you think you know, don't you? You think you know what this one is about, don't you? You think I'm, more or less, directly saying that my sister, Emma, is a big baby who flounces around the place, barks orders at me, makes corporate strategic decisions without the merest hint of a consultation with the *founder of the company*, makes me do things that I don't want to do because my way "doesn't make sense" and is generally annoying in a way that only little sisters can be. That's what you're thinking, yeah? That's what you think this poem is about.

Well, guys, you're wrong, yeah?

And, no. I'm not winking at you.

WINK

LOL

OFFICIAL STATEMENT BY EMMA MATREEZ

Hello,

Before I continue, I just want to clarify that this isn't a poem called "Official Statement by Emma Matreez". Instead it is literally an official statement by me, Emma Matreez, CEO of Cheeky Monkey HD.com Industries.

I'm sorry to interupt your 'enjoyment' of this 'book', but as the Publisher of the aforementioned 'book' I think I'm well within my rights to respond to the previous 'poem'. Plus, as the Publisher of said 'book' nobody can stop me having my say, even if I didn't have the right.

Basically, he's an idiot, isn't he? Apparently I'm the 'big baby', but I'm not the one who's written a poem moaning about how rubbish it is to have to listen to the opinions of your boss who is also your sister, am I?

That's all I really wanted to say.

Bye. x

Although this isn't a poem and wasn't written by me, I'm still going to go ahead and analyse it.

(Hi Guys, it's me, Cheeky Monkey HD.com, here, by the way)

This 'Emma Matreez' character, whoever she is[1], really is full of herself, isn't she? What sort of narcissist would hijack a prestige author's precious pages to insert their own conspiracy theory laden diatribe upon an unsuspecting public?[2]

The only thing we can take away from this 'statement' is that I'm sure she must have a long-suffering elder sibling who is some kind of artistic genius.[3]

Gordon's gin

Got knocked over

He wasn't happy

His attachment

To this drink

Worried his wife

Gordon's Gin is the name of a popular brand of gin, but in this instance I've used wordology to transform this into it being a specific glass of generic gin that is being drunk by a guy called Gordon.

As a poem, it's not up to much, but in a more general sense: if drinking is becoming a problem for you then please seek help.

REALLY?

Garfield

Big fat ginger cat

Purely a coincidence

Claimed owner

Some people.

"Oh, that's an unusual name you've given your baby. Did you name him after the footballer of the same name, who plays for the team you support and you have a poster of them in your house despite you being a grown adult who is really too old to have a poster of a footballer in your house?"

"No. I just like the name."

Some people.

THE KEYS TO SUCCESS

Take That!

screamed Gary Barlow

Of Take That fame

Squash racket rampant

Squash quaffed orangely

Squash cooked with butter and nuts

Barlow does not play.

He acts.

Gary "Gazza" Barlow is the cuddly, unsexy one, yeah? Get real - there's steel behind those eyes. And it's steel carefully crafted into a baseball bat.

Gary displayed his ruthless streak as a teenager when he cut off his father, Ken, who he has never spoken to since (apparently he wouldn't promote an early gig of Gary's in the Weatherfield Gazette). Intoxicated by the sheer rush of merciless energy, Gazza went on to be known as the 'Don' of the pop world due to his relentless pursuit of success via a string of hit singles and his insistence on not speaking to his dad.

Some people still think that Ronnie Williams escaped untarnished from Gazza's orbit and became the successful one because he did that song about angels (can't remember what it was called). But where is Ronnie Williams now? I'll tell you: he's sat in his undies watching old videos on a laptop.

Where's Gazza now? Playing squash, drinking squash, eating (butternut) squash. i.e. living his best life.

Note: Being called 'Don' in no way relates to Don Brennan who lived in the same street as Barlow when he were a lad.

BATTLE OF WITS

The poem bragged

"I don't need to rhyme"

"I can shoot off wildly"

"Then turn on a dime"

The writer smiled

"But I want you to rhyme"

"It's more structurally coherent"

"And accessible to readers"

Meh.

Giant, warm, fluffy

Naan bread

Sleeping bag size

Sleeping bag function

Breakfast included

Are there any Dragons out there interested in this?

By Dragons, I'm talking about the annoying 'business person on the telly' variety, rather than the flame-breathing monster type. I'm looking for someone to invest in the concept, not to use their natural flame breath to naturally char aforementioned breads.

That said, if any giant flame-breathing dragons want to invest in my 'giant naan bread as a sleeping bag' business then I'm not prejudiced and I'm happy to take on any offers. I'm looking for £275,000 for a 5% share.

Many thanks.

Kenneth Pilchards' granddaughter was headhunted by an international conglomerate of fake award manufacturers. She declined their advances and returned to her work as a holistic vocal coach. Kennth was proud of her resolve, but quietly mourned his one chance to access cost price fake awards.

This is very much a stroll through the garden of 'slice of life' poetry. Can you smell Kenneth's flower? Do you want to water his granddaughter's sense of self, perhaps mow the lawn that is the managing director of the fake award manufacturers? Create a path from Kenneth's secret anguish?

These feelings of wanting to apply gardening techniques to the subjects of a poem are very much the raison d'être of the slice of life genre. Was it not Monty Don himself that said: "Gizza a look at your poem, la"?

It probably wasn't him, to be honest. I don't remember him being Scouse.

Deirdre Take longed for

Her daughter to find

Her hand taken

In marriage

To that end:

Experimental Daughter Enlargening Ray

Big Miss Take

In this poem I have cleverly combined the following trinity of concepts: busybody mothers, science fiction, and Julia Roberts' catchphrase.

I can't say for sure, but I'm pretty certain that I'm the only poet that's ever attempted to do so, so to achieve such success on the first attempt is pretty impressive and, I would have thought, should qualify me for some kind of poetry lifetime achievement award.

That said, if you know of any other poems that *successfully* combine this trio of ideas then I'm happy to read and review, then assess my place within their pantheon. However, I will insist on proof of when these poems were originally written as I do not want to fall victim to a bandwagon jumping scenario.

"Let's Jam,"

Said the strawberry

To their bandmates:

Plum, raspberry and damson.

Think about it... jam, right?

Lovely, lovely jam. Preferably on toast.

Tenderstem Broccoli

Could be the name

Of a complex protagonist

Of an equally complex

Literary novel

I might write it

If I'm honest, this is more of a 'note to self' than it is a poem in its own right. But that's fine, OK? Poems come in all shapes and sizes, even if that shape and/or size is 'not really a poem'.

It's a pretty good idea, though, isn't it? Please don't mention it to anybody. I'd be heartbroken if it was stolen.

My darling...are you there?

Yes! I'm down here!

Good poetry doesn't just rely on words and their meaning. It also leverages the scientific power of position.

Until Steve Guttenberg invented his infamous 'press', words could literally appear on a page at literally any time. It made writing almost impossible and reading a downright chore. Very occasionally it would work out, like the time that Shakespeare wrote that play about a monkey with a typewriter, but that was luck and luck only.

People say he was a genius, but I'd like to see how he would get on post-invention of the printing press. Just to *prove* that luck wasn't a factor. The plays would still have probably been great, but we'll never know for sure.

Lucky, lucky Shakespeare.

Click clack

Train track

Click clack

Chewing gum smack

Click clack

Rhythmic attack

Click clack

Shut up, Jack!

Kids are annoying. They insist on repeatedly doing something (generally involving making a noise) over and over again until your brain just screams: "Stop doing that will you?" It's never entirely clear whether they're just doing it because they like it and they're unaware that it's annoying, or whether they know it's annoying and that's why they're enjoying it. Either way: it's annoying.

Further thoughts:

1) This would make a terrific bit of stand up comedy.
2) By kids, I'm mainly thinking of Emma, who, at this point, is actually an adult
3) My niece, Eva, is pretty much the only kid I know and she's not remotely annoying, so I think it really is just her mum.

Can dogs drink coffee?

Enquired Derek

Only artisanal roasts

Replied the suspiciously inexpensive vet

Derek sighed and decided that next time he'd return to the regular surgery

As a world-renowned pet owner, I just want to say that, yes, it's a 'dear-do' to go to the vets, but please don't fall for any of these backstreet, cheapo vets that are all the rage these days. I honestly doubt that they have *any* relevant qualifications.

Do you have a napkin?

A serviette?

A little tissue?

Asked Audrey.

No

Replied her browbeaten husband.

Wiping sweat from his maw

With an old hankie

Slice of life again, innit. I'm not a married guy, but this is the kind of thing that I imagine happens to married guys. As a poet, I'm happy to leave it in the realm of 'this is what I imagine a particular type of life to be', and I will not research the matter any further, as the only options available that I can see are:

1. Yes, this is what married life is like and that's depressing.
2. No, this isn't what married life is like and I might be missing out on something good.

Yes, I do feel better

Exclaimed Mcalmont

And/or

Butler.

That's great

Replied the doctor

I won't need to see you for another year

This took a bit of a dark turn, if I'm honest, and I'm *really* not aiming to be one of the depressing poets. I hope that McAlmont and/or Butler are doing fine. I won't Google them, just in case.

Sakura Miyuki-Kun boarded the Shinkansen, which promptly left on time. Ensconced in his seat and surveying the carriage, he observed an American tourist furiously ranting after discovering that the train wasn't an actual bullet.

"Tsk, absolutely typical," he would have said to himself had he not been Japanese.

This feels like I'm having a go at someone, but I'm not. Well, I don't think I am. I might be, but, if I am, it's purely subconscious and I apologise in advance.

Would an American really think that a bullet train is a literal bullet? I'm not sure. Would a Japanese person have been having a nosey around a train carriage? It's more likely that they would have kept themselves to themself.

The question that nobody is asking is this: where is the Shinkansen going to?

It's Osaka.

Dawn French Spaniel

Jarvis Cocker Spaniel

Jerry Springer Spaniel

Vauxhall Cavalier King Charles Spaniel

Kooikerhondje!

Kooikerhondje is a real make of spaniel! Unbelievable. I just had to share this information and I concocted this poem around it in order to do so.

Poetry has utility as well as being word-based decoration. You'd do well to remember that, guys.

FUN FACT: This is the second poem of the book to mention spaniels.

NRG1

No Repeat Guarantee

Announces Radio station

Periodically

Exactly

And identically

All throughout the day

Just seems ironic, you know? A little *too* ironic, doncha think? Yeah, I really do think.

I know that they mean that they won't play the same songs during any given day, but even so: kind of interesting.

Again, this would make a terrific bit of stand up material.

NRG2

Radio station's

No Repeat Guarantee

Is

Fundamental physical property

Screams headline

Upon consulting the original paper:

Although true at a quantum level, the effect quickly dissipates when applied at the macro level.

I've got to say that the science involved in this poem is totally beyond me and I had to consult with several 'top boffins' in order to ensure that my speculations were accurate as well as being artistically gratifying.

None of them got back to me, so I just had to release it into the wild, as is.

Fingers crossed.

Unions meet with management representatives at the C&C Music Factory to discuss pay and conditions. Workers believe that the number of notes they're being asked to process doesn't comply with safety regulations. There is a risk that a rogue clef could impale a passing kitten. Management agree to additional 15 minute break and the strike is broken: Everybody Dance Now

I've just painted a mind painting. Deal with it, bitches.

Guys, I wouldn't normally dream of using the word 'bitches' but the phrase "Deal with it, bitches" was the only phrase that I felt conveyed an adequate level of stank on the situation.

Now, Guys, I wouldn't normally dream of using the word 'stank' in this context, given the connotations of a past tense 'stink', but, as a world renowned writer, I am continually pushing myself into realms hitherto unvisited.

Regardless, I have painted a mind painting and you're both looking at it and living in it.

UNEXPECTED CELEBRITY FAMILIES

Chuck and his wife, Mary, enjoy one of her delicious meals and reminisce about the many childhood mishaps caused by son Matt's luxurious voice.

Siblings Warren and Gina fondly remember father Dustin and the hilarious impressions he would perform for them as children.

Bryan visits France to reconnect with long lost brother, Cross Channel.

I don't think any of them are really related (I've not checked), but surely the power of poetry is that whence one can create it thusly?

As the water balloon exploded

Graham quipped

"More like Dame Judi *Drenched*"

The assembled dignitaries tutted

Graham was quickly

Whisked away

Come *on*, Graham, she's an old woman. Getting soaked by the, presumably, cold water in a water balloon is potentially lethal. Some people will risk *anything* in order to get their stupid joke in.

Bruce Forsyth
Went to Gloucester
Except it wasn't him
Just a clever imposter

Fake Bruce's scam
Contained layer upon layer
He'd go to the council
And become the new mayor

He appeared in town
With a confident grin
A competent tap dance
And a stick-on chin

What a disgrace!
I hope he gets what he's due!
To find out what happens,
Please read Part 2

Let me give you a peek behind my curtain. This poem wasn't really the first part of a two part *duology*. No, it was simply the beginning part of a slightly longer 'singleology'. Unfortunately, the length of this unified poem was longer than one page, and that would mean a significant breach to the ongoing *'format du jour'* of this very magnificent work of art that thou art holding/reading.

I'm not the sort of poet who would let such a minor speed-bump curb my excessive driving style. I'm the sort of poet who would thrust my foot deeper into the accelerator pedal and take that speed-bump on with full force; to the extent that I've ruined my suspension and end up having to take it into the garage.

Basically, I've just split it in two and added a cliffhanger element. Let's go read Part 2…

BRUCE FORSTYTH IMPERSONATOR (PART 2 OF 2)

Part 2 has commenced
Let's reach our conclusion
And yank this imposter
From his dangerous delusion
His plan fell apart
With a vigorous cough
Fake Bruce fell over
And his chin fell off
Ashamed to his core
By this epic fail
His reflection ran deep
On the moral to this tale:

If you impersonate Brucie
You'll soon pay the price
It's nice to see you
To see you nice

Right, I can do the real analysis now.

Just the thought of someone attempting to leverage the reputation of Sir Bruce, built with over 70 years of hard work, for some kind of petty political gain, is enough to make my blood boil. Quite literally (it's a medical condition).

This poem is my attempt to persuade anybody thinking of taking such a heinous action to think again and not take such a heinous action.

Notification to the

Man in the Vauxhall Corsa

With the Jesus fish symbol

Stuck to the boot

(of your Vauxhall Corsa)

Have you considered whether or not Jesus

Would approve of your vehicular choice?

He'd probably prefer it if you walked

Or use a donkey

From what I've been told

He was like an old fashioned hippy

In this poem I play the role of agent provocateur in that I challenge the values of a Christian, but not in the sense that I am a fancy pair of knickers.

I hope that the Vauxhall Corsa guy doesn't spend too long thinking about it. I think that J-Dogg (Jesus) would likely be fine with the Corsa, especially if it's an electric one. It's these pricks in those unnecessarily massive cars who are going straight to hell.

The End

This isn't a poem. It's literally the end of the book.

Or maybe it *is* a poem.

At this point, you're surely qualified enough to decide for yourself...

OTHER STUFF ALSO BY ME

Hi Guys, it's me, Cheeky Monkey HD.com, here, in a post-credits sequence in which I plan to enlighten you as to some of the other projects in which I have creatively dabbled (or dabbled creatively, depending on your preference).

Normalman's Fate is an animated drama series that appears on the *Very Cheeky Productions* Youtube channel. John Normalman is the most successful Business Guy in town until his wanton lack of respect for common decency sees him transported to a magical realm. Will he learn the error of his ways and travel home? Will his wife, Sandra, make any friends? And what does President Darren Goghulbochs have to do with it all? Just watch the fantastic 12 episodes and find out.

The Cheeky Monkey HD.Podcast is my (Cheeky Monkey HD.com) podcast. It's not really *about* anything per se, but it's kind of fun. Have a listen if you want. Or watch it, cos it's also on Youtube. Or don't. It's up to you.

All my wares may be tracked via my web-site, which is, conveniently, the same as my name:

https://www.cheekymonkeyhd.com

JOSE'S PAGE

Hello. I am Jose.
(You say it like Mourinho, not like one of the Spanish people who is also called it.)
I am an employee of this company and I usually have to do the tasks that the boss doesn't want to do. Or sometimes the ones that he can't be bothered to do. Sometimes it is hard to tell which one of those is which.
I am here to talk to you fans about the things that you want to do and talk about and see in future projects by the boss. I don't really have much to say this time, as nobody has said anything to me from what I can respond to. Why not chuck us an email and then next time I might have something to talk to you about:

jose@cheekymonkeyhd.com

Ta,
Jose

---

[1] She's my sister, unfortunately.

[2] My sister is that sort of narcissist.

[3] I'm talking about me! lol

Printed in Great Britain
by Amazon

37501060R00050